MAKE ME LAUGH!

MONSTER MAYHEM

Jokes to Scare You Silly!

by Sam Schultz
pictures by Brian Gable

Carolrhoda Books, Inc. • Minneapolis

First Mother Monster: You have the ugliest baby I've ever seen.

Second Mother Monster: Thank you very much!

Q: How do you tell a good monster from a bad one?

A: If you meet a good monster, you'll be able to talk about it later!

Q: What did the mother ghost say to her son when they got into the car?

A: Be sure to fasten your sheet belt.

Ad in monster newspaper: "Use Mummy Soap for that School-Ghoul complexion."

Q: What kind of banks do vampires go to?

A: Blood banks.

Q: Where would you find a one-handed monster?

A: In a second-hand store.

Monster (to gas station man): Fill me up.

Gas Station Man: You have to have a car first!

Monster: But I had a car for lunch!

First Monster: I'm on a seafood diet.

Second Monster: What do you eat?

First Monster: Whatever I see!

Q: Did you hear about the vampire's coffin?

A: He stopped after he took a cough drop.

A vampire agreed to go to Hollywood to star in a movie when the director offered him a role he could really sink his teeth into!

Q: What do you get when you cross a monster with a computer?

A: A 500-pound genius.

Witch Hazel: Wilma, did you put the cat out?

Witch Wilma: Why? Is it on fire?

Q: How do you greet a three-headed monster?

A: Hello! Hello! Hello! How are you? How are you? How are you?

First Astronaut: What has 6 eyes, 10 arms, and is green all over?

Second Astronaut: I don't know.

First Astronaut: I don't know, either, but it's looking in our window!

Q: Why was the monster afraid to leave his house?

A: He didn't like what he read in his horrorscope.

Q: What do you do with a green monster?

A: Put it in the sun until it ripens.

Child Monster: Mama, I have a stomachache.

Mother Monster: It must be someone you ate.

Q: Pretend you're surrounded by 50 werewolves and 30 vampires. What would you do?

A: I'd stop pretending!

First Monster: I'm starved!

Second Monster: Dinner is thawing in the refrigerator.

First Monster: Oh good. Who is it?

A fiery dragon captured a knight in armor. The knight begged the dragon to be kind to him because he hadn't had a bite in three days. So the dragon bit him!

Q: Who would name a monster King Tut?

A: His mummy.

First Monster: Am I late for dinner?

Second Monster: Yes, everyone's been eaten.

Q: Did you hear about the football game between the Dallas Cowboys and a team of monsters?

A: Yeah, the Cowboys were eaten alive!

Q: What steps would you take if a monster was about to attack you?

A: Long ones!

Q: What happened to the monster who ate the electric company?

A: He was in shock for a week.

Jenny and Tommy were playing ball. A monster walked up to them and asked, "What time is it?"

"Time to run!" said Jenny and Tommy.

Q: Why do witches fly around on broomsticks?

A: Because they're cheaper than airplanes.

Q: Why are vampires like stars?

A: Because they only come out at night.

Q: Why don't monsters cross the road?

A: Because they don't want to be mistaken for chickens.

Q: By which lake is there a monster motel?

A: Lake Erie.

First Monster: What's this we're eating?

Second Monster: Ladyfingers.

First Monster: They're delicious. I hope the rest of the lady tastes this good!

Q: What did the vampire catch after staying up all night?

A: A bat cold.

Young Frankenstein's monstrous
   invention
Caused trouble too awful to mention.
His actions were ghoulish,
Which proves it is foolish
To monkey with Nature's intention!

Q: What did the monster say to his blind date?

A: You look good enough to eat.

Q: Did you hear about the cookie monster who almost drowned?

A: He tried to dunk himself in a vat of milk.

First Monster: You mean you went to college, but you still eat your victims?

Second Monster: Yes, but now I use a knife and a fork!

Q: Why did the monster fall in love with a piano?

A: Because it had such beautiful straight teeth.

Sheriff: Did you see a monster take this road a short time ago?

Young Man: No, the road is still here.

Q: What's the best thing to do if you meet a blue monster?

A: Cheer him up.

Mary Monster: George is a real dummy.

Alice Monster: Why do you say that?

Mary Monster: He can't count to 40 without taking his shoes off!

Q: Did you hear the new werewolf band last Saturday?

A: Yes, it was a howling success.

A monster adrift on a raft
Had never been on such a craft.
He fashioned a sail
With his body and tail,
While the fishes around him just
    laughed.

Q: What do you call a monster who ate
his mother's sister?

A: An aunt-eater.

Knight Teacher: How can you keep a
dragon from charging?

Knight Student: By taking away his
credit card.

Q: What kind of werewolves never
need ironing?

A: Wash and werewolves.

Joe: What's the difference between a monster and a watermelon?

Moe: I don't know.

Joe: Well, then I'll never send you to the store for a watermelon!

First Vampire: I called the gang and told them we're playing cards at the cemetery tonight.

Second Vampire: Why there?

First Vampire: Well, if someone doesn't show, we can always dig up another player.

Q: What's big and mean and only eats candy rocks?

A: The Big Rock Candy Monster.

Q: What must a ghost buy before he can scare anyone?

A: A haunting license.

Q: What do you get when you cross a monster with a parrot?

A: I don't know. But when it talks, you'd better listen!

Q: Did you hear about the monster rock band?

A: They played to screaming audiences every night!

Q: What's green, weighs 2,000 pounds, and has 8 wheels?

A: A monster on roller skates.

Q: What's the best way to approach an evil-eyed monster?

A: Very carefully!

Q: Why didn't the vampire want to play baseball?

A: Because he didn't want to damage his bats.

Girl Monster: You must think I'm a perfect idiot.

Boy Monster: No, of course not. Nobody's perfect!

A fire-breathing monster in Spain
Woke up with a terrible pain.
It wasn't his dream
That caused him to scream.
He had set his huge tail aflame!

Q: Did you hear about the new vampire delivery service?

A: It's a fly-by-night operation!

Mary: I just saw a monster with 60 arms, and I didn't even run.

Gary: Weren't you scared?

Mary: Nah! He didn't have a leg to stand on.

Monster mother to child: I told you never to speak with someone in your mouth!

First Vampire: You're a pain in the neck.

Second Vampire: Thank you for the compliment!

Mother Cannibal: Junior was sent home from school today.

Father Cannibal: Why, what did he do?

Mother Cannibal: He tried to butter up his teacher!

First Monster: You don't have a brain in your head.

Second Monster: Which head?

Two sea monsters had just finished eating a fisherman. "You know," said one to the other, "I'd like fishermen a lot better if they didn't have so many bones."

Q: Why doesn't Dracula trust the Invisible Man?

A: Because he can see right through him.

Child Monster: Mama, may I eat New York City?

Mother Monster: Only if you wash your hands first.

Q: What does Dracula do when the sun comes up?

A: He takes a coffin break.

Q: Why did the vampire call the morgue?

A: He wanted to see if they delivered.

Lou: Never play catch with a 5,000-pound monster.

Sue: Why not?

Lou: Because they're very, very heavy!

Q: Did you hear about the bald-headed man who met a man-eating monster?

A: He had a hair-raising experience!

Don: Three monsters were arrested for throwing a party.

Ron: Why?

Don: They threw it over the Grand Canyon!

Q: Why aren't vampires welcome in blood banks?

A: Because they only make withdrawals.

First Monster: A nice family moved next door to me.

Second Monster: I hope they'll be people you can enjoy.

First Monster: Enjoy? I think they'll be delicious!

Q: Why did the vampires ask a ghost to join their football team?

A: Because they needed some team spirit.

Q: Where did the witch keep her flying machine?

A: In the br-r-r-oom closet.

Q: What do monsters have that no one else can have?

A: Baby monsters!

Q: What's the best way to talk to a people-eating monster?

A: By long distance!

Tommy Ghost: Mother, can I join the army?

Mother Ghost: No, but you can join the Ghost Guard.

Q: What's red and white on the outside and green and lumpy on the inside?

A: A can of Cream of Monster soup.

First Monster: Where are you going?

Second Monster: I'm going to school.

First Monster: Why don't you take a bus?

Second Monster: Nah. My mom will only make me take it back.

Q: What do sea monsters eat for dinner?

A: Fish and ships.

Q: Do vampires have holidays?

A: Sure, haven't you ever heard of Fangsgiving Day?

Q: Why did the little girl monster eat a box of bullets?

A: She wanted to grow bangs.

Mother Monster: Do you think we should take Junior to the zoo?

Father Monster: Certainly not! If the zoo wants Junior, they can come and get him!

Q: What do you call a city that monsters live in?

A: A monstrosity (Monstro-city).

A giant green monster from Blister
Decided to eat up his sister,
And when he was through
He cried, "What did I do?"
Now he's sorry he did, 'cause he
  missed her.

Mother Monster: Son, I thought I told you to drink your medicine after your hot bath.

Son Monster: I'm sorry, Mom. But after I finished drinking the bath, I couldn't drink another drop!

Monster Doctor: What seems to be the trouble?

Monster Patient: I don't know. I feel upset.

Monster Doctor: Well, maybe you're just fed up with people.

Dan: Why did the monster paint his toes red?

Jan: I don't know. Why?

Dan: So he could hide in a cherry tree.

Jan: I've never seen a monster in a cherry tree.

Dan: See? It works!

Mother monster to child: How many times must I tell you to play with your food before you eat it?

Tim: Why do monsters have square shoulders?

Jim: Because they eat lots of cereal.

Tim: How can cereal give them square shoulders?

Jim: It's not the cereal. It's the boxes!

Q: Why do dragons sleep in the daytime?

A: So they can hunt knights.

First Monster: We must be in a city.

Second Monster: What makes you think so?

First Monster: We're stepping on more people!

Child Monster: Here's a present for you.

Mother Monster: Thank you. It's beautiful.

Child Monster: I made it with my own ten hands!

Secretary: Mr. Jones, the Invisible Man is here to see you.

Mr. Jones: Tell him I can't possibly see him.

Carolrhoda Books, Inc.,
A division of Lerner Publishing Group
241 First Avenue North
Minneapolis, MN 55401 U.S.A.

Website address: www.lernerbooks.com

Library of Congress Cataloging-in-Publication Data

Schultz, Sam.
    Monster mayhem : jokes to scare you silly / by Sam Schultz ;
illustrations by Brian Gable.
        p.   cm. — (Make me laugh)
    Summary: A collection of jokes about monsters.
    ISBN: 1–57505–642–9 (lib. bdg. : alk. paper)
    ISBN: 1–57505–708–5 (pbk. : alk. paper)
    1. Monsters—Juvenile humor. [1. Monsters—Humor. 2. Jokes. 3. Riddles.
4. Puns and punning.] I. Gable, Brian, 1949– ill. II. Title. III. Series.
    PN6231.M665 S33 2004
    818'.5402—dc21   2002151107

Manufactured in the United States of America
2 3 4 5 6 7 – JR – 10 09 08 07 06 05